MW00736484

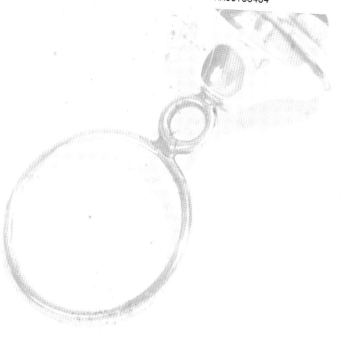

CHIC

Components

"It sometimes happens, even
in the best of families, that a baby is born.
This is not necessarily cause for
alarm. The important thing is to keep
your wits about you and borrow
some money."

ELINOR GOULDING SMITH

CHIC
SIMPLE®
Components

N U R S E R Y

ALFRED A. KNOPF NEW YORK 1994

THIS IS A BORZOI BOOK
PUBLISHED BY ALFRED A. KNOPF, INC.

KIM JOHNSON GROSS   JEFF STONE

WRITTEN BY RACHEL URQUHART
PHOTOGRAPHS BY DANA GALLAGHER
STYLED BY BECKY McDERMOTT

ART DIRECTION BY WAYNE WOLF
ICON ILLUSTRATION BY ERIC HANSON

Library of Congress Cataloging-in-Publication Data
Urquhart, Rachel
Chic Simple components. Nursery / [written by Rachel Urquhart; edited by Kim
Johnson Gross, Jeff Stone]. — 1st ed.
p. cm.
ISBN 0-679-43221-3
1. Nurseries—Equipment and supplies I. Gross, Kim Johnson.
II. Stone, Jeff, [date]. III. Title. IV. Title: Nursery.
HQ784.N8U77 1994
843'.53—dc20
94-25666
CIP

Manufactured in the United States of America
First Edition

CONTENTS

"The more you know, the less you need."

AUSTRALIAN ABORIGINAL SAYING

CHIC
SIMPLE ®

Chic Simple is a primer for living well but sensibly. It's for those who believe that quality of life does not come in accumulating things, but in paring down to the essentials. Chic Simple enables readers to bring value and style into their lives with economy and simplicity.

N U R S E R Y

It is the first room your child will know—his or her introduction to the world outside the womb. For nine long months before your baby's dramatic entrance, it is the room you imagine, erase, then reimagine. Memories of your own childhood take hold—the sights that made you smile, the smells that comforted you, the sounds you imagine you liked to hear. You pore over catalogues and brave bewildering trips to baby stores. You wonder, Can anything be soft enough, safe enough, good enough for this amazing about-to-be being? And why is everything so ugly?

"Wanted: Playpen, cot and high chair. Also two single beds."

Advertisement in The Evening Standard

THE HISTORY OF NURSERIES

ORIGINATED WITH THE FIRST CRIES OF

THE VICTORIAN AGE, WHEN CHILDREN WERE TO BE "seen and not heard." It was, literally, the nurse's room. Turn-of-the-century British houses had entire children's wings, with night and day nurseries, a kitchen, and bath. Apart from elaborate infant cradles and bassinets, the furniture was adult furniture, the legs cut down to toddler size. As nurseries became more fashionable, they existed as stylized monuments to the wealth of the parents, stuffed full of expensive adult things—lace, satin, appliqué, fancy furnishings. Postwar hardship brought an end to such lavishness, and the nursery evolved into a room that was centered entirely on the child. As such, it reflected a fundamental shift in attitudes toward children: no longer mere display objects to be styled and shown off accordingly, they were seen as individuals, who needed surroundings that reflected their personalities.

"Having children is like having a bowling alley installed in your brain."

MARTIN MULL

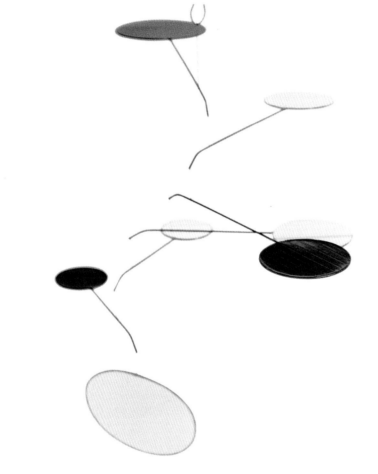

Stimuli. SIGHT. Infants can focus on objects between eight and fifteen inches away. By one month, they can see three feet and track moving targets. At three months, they can smile halfway across the room at you! Their long-range and color vision matures around four months. Their favorite sight? Mom's or Dad's face. SOUND. They don't need silence, though sudden loud noises may frighten them or make them shut down. They prefer rhythmic sounds, music, the babble of a familiar voice. The sound of a running faucet, the hum of a washing machine, even a car engine may calm their cries and put them to sleep. Their favorite sound? Mom's or Dad's voice. TOUCH. The warmth of your skin and the feeling of being enfolded in your arms are the most potent forms of stimulation they feel. This will calm them like nothing else. Swaddling them tightly in a flannel receiving blanket combines soothing warmth with firm pressure and containment. Gentle massage gets them used to being touched.

Safety. It obsesses you. Radiators have no use other than to burn tiny hands. Doors exist simply to trap fingers. And stairs? You never realized it before, but they were invented for the sole purpose of luring and tripping up innocent toddlers. The obvious solution is to move into a dark, one-story padded cell. But first, try baby-proofing. See the world as your child does. Wires are for teething on and electrical outlets are for sticking wet fingers into. Stop them up with safety plugs. Mr. Clean looks like lemonade. Put it out of reach and lock it up. Window guards, where not required by law, should be required by logic.

The Consumer Reports Guide to Baby Products *will tell you just how unsafe baby-proofing products can be. A brief roundup: No pressure-mounted gates at the top or bottom of stairways—they can give way. No accordion gates whatsoever—they can trap tiny heads and necks. Expandable, accordion-style enclosures? Same problem. Outlet plugs should be secure and too big to swallow if pried loose. Don't get cabinet latches a professional safe-cracker would have trouble with—you'll end up not bothering to close them. Conversely, give babies credit: they are, essentially, doughy Houdinis.*

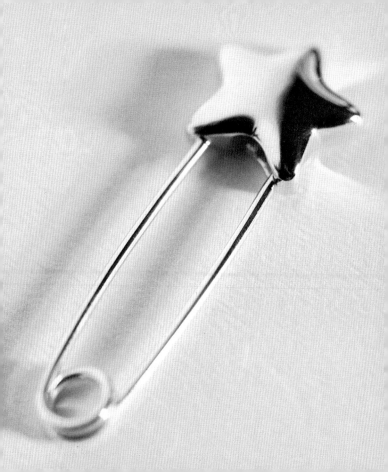

Comfort. The nursery is a womb with a view. Instead of warm amniotic fluid, your newborn rests on soft, even, unbleached sheets, swaddled in warm blankets and surrounded by a cushioned bumper. It doesn't need to be in the quietest part of the house. After all, your baby's last piece of real estate looked out over your stomach: how peaceful do you think that was? It may not even be a separate room—just a cozy corner equipped with the bare essentials. In fact, babies often feel safer if they can hear voices outside their door. Soft toys and musical pillows are ideal for crib-play. A pacifier—if you're not aesthetically opposed—can calm even the most beastly of babies. A favorite doll, blanket, or piece of Mom's clothing can make a strange bed feel like home. But true comfort comes with security and routine—and the soothing knowledge that Mom and Dad are never more than a healthy scream away.

Changes. It's true: they grow. What started as a seemingly helpless creature the size of a football is suddenly a bubbly, willful person about to take his first steps. Nurseries have to grow up too. Cribs should have adjustable mattress heights (four settings is standard). That beautiful antique standing lamp may have been perfect while your baby was immobile. Now he shakes it like a coconut tree. Get rid of it. Start with plenty of extra space or boxes for storage—it'll make the unavoidable accumulation of stuff (toys, baby paraphernalia, more toys—and oh, did we mention toys?) easier to bear. Resign yourself to the inevitable: the nursery isn't your room—it's his.

TEETHING

Teething can make your baby—and you— miserable. The signs? Drool—lots of it. Irritability. Runny nose. Refusal to feed. Ear-pulling and cheek-rubbing. Low fever. Diarrhea. What helps? Something to chew on: frozen bananas are great. A washcloth with an ice cube wrapped tightly secured with a rubber band. Teething rings, especially the kind you can freeze, or the ones with bumps on them. Rub your finger on their gums. Feed them cold food, like yogurt. If all else fails, try pain relief (Infants' Tylenol) but check with your pediatrician first.

Simple Nursery. With its mangers and woven baskets, the Bible has this concept down pat. (Little did Moses know his name would someday be associated with expensive portable baby carriers.) When the hand-me-downs, the advice, the baby showers, the catalogues, the excessive list-making, the decorating, the cleaning...when it all starts to get to you, remember this: your baby needs food, some sort of diaper, and a clean comfortable place to sleep. That's it. A bureau drawer lined with soft clothes will do just fine. A basket with handles, a mattress, cloth lining, linens, and a blanket is even better—it's lightweight, comfortable, and portable. It was good enough for Moses. It'll probably work for junior.

"A baby is an angel whose wings decrease as his legs increase."

FRENCH PROVERB

C L O T H E S

Babies don't wear clothes so much as pass through them. That cute frock with the daisies? It's the teddy bear's now. Buy large. Buy now for later. Think about the seasons: it's great to pick up a snowsuit on sale— just remember that your child may have doubled in size before the next snowflakes appear. What's important for you to think about? Comfort. Washability. Easy on, easy off. Diaper access. Economy. Durability. Style.

"An ugly baby is a very nasty object, and the prettiest is frightful when undressed."

QUEEN VICTORIA

Diapers. Disposable vs. cloth. Manufacturers of disposable diapers claim that cloth diapers are unsanitary (untrue), promote diaper rash (untrue), and pollute the environment more than disposables do (also untrue). Cloth diaper enthusiasts will tell you it's much cheaper (true if you wash them yourself; not true if you use a service) and it doesn't pollute as much (true: over 16 billion disposables end up in landfills each year). Cloth diapers become saturated more quickly than disposable ones, so your choice matters most at night, when frequent diaper changes might disrupt his sleep and yours. So be environmentally correct by day, and use a disposable at night.

DUMPSTER

Newborns use about 12 diapers per day; a toddler child uses about 6, but needs more absorbency.

No more stiff plastic pants. Get diaper covers with waterproof liners and comfortable cotton or soft wool on the outside—they fasten with Velcro over cloth diapers. For heavy wetters and nighttime diapering, flannel liners increase absorbency.

Newborn. If newborns could talk about fashion, they'd tell you to keep them in their birthday suits and wrap them in your arms. But since nakedness can be impractical in the cold, dry world they've been thrust into, soft cotton comes in handy. Don't bother with newborn sizes—you'll be buying three-to-six-month sizes within a few weeks of coming home. Clothes should go on easily. Stretch neck holes open before pulling them over your baby's head. "Onesies" that snap at the crotch and "stretchies" are the most practical, comfortable clothes. Cover tiny feet with socks and booties— infants have notoriously bad circulation.

TO BLEACH OR
NOT TO BLEACH
A newborn's skin reacts to strong detergents. Wash everything your infant comes into contact with in a mild, no-bleach detergent like Ivory or Dreft. You can rinse it twice if you're worried there may be soap left in it. Separating out your baby's clothing from your own is unnecessary, unless you're particularly fond of groundhog-sized piles of laundry. Treat stains with spot remover rather than throw a lot of bleach into the machine. Soaking in water with lemon juice or white vinegar brightens things up considerably.

"Preceded only by food, clothing is a child's earliest opportunity to exercise personal autonomy."

MARILISE
FLUSSER

Toddler. "To toddle," according to the *Oxford English Dictionary,* is "to walk or run with short unsteady steps, as a child just beginning to walk." Toddlers demand a lot from their clothes: that they be durable, that they be unrestrictive, that they accommodate an uneasy relationship with the forces of gravity. It's no wonder overalls reign supreme. Keep things comfortable. Keep things accessible. (European clothes are beautiful, but with no leg snaps, they're often hard to put on.) Above all, keep things light and let your kid call a few of the shots: just because you enjoy dressing like a German film director doesn't mean your one-year-old will.

SNAP AWAY

As a new parent, prepare to worship at the altar of the snap. Without them, changing a diaper would be like alligator wrestling. With their help, it can be done practically at lightspeed. As to the right number, long-legged pants, overalls, or pajamas should have at least six. Eight is perfect.

Summer. You remember what it's like. Ice-cream trucks. Sprinklers. The beach. The playground. Staying cool and protected from the sun is still the point. Bring bottles of water with you when you go out: dehydration is a real danger in the heat. Applying baby cornstarch after a tepid bath soothes heat rash. Rubber-soled sandals help keep tiny feet from frying. Lightweight T-shirts and shorts with patterns are easier to keep clean—and to spot in a crowded playground. Overalls with nothing but a diaper and sunscreen underneath look as good now as they did sixty years ago. Sun hats with brims or visors shield young faces.

PALEFACE

Babies should wear sunscreen like a second skin, but look for a high SPF (at least SPF 15) that screens out UVB and UVA rays. PABA, heavy fragrance, and colorings can cause allergic reactions: make a patch test the first time you use a product, then wait 24 hours. Look for products especially designed for babies. Limit time spent in the sun, no matter how strong your sunscreen is.

" Of all animals,
the boy is the most
unmanageable."

PLATO

Winter. Sniffles, chapped faces, snow glare—the cold is tough on babies. Keep snowsuits as easy to get in and out of as possible (full-length zippers are the key). Hats should be soft, not itchy, and should fasten over the ears and under the chin. Ski masks are for muggers—and babies on bitter cold days. Attempting to thread gloves onto tiny toddler hands can try even the best-natured soul. Mittens with no fingers at all are the simplest to slip on. Attach them with old-fashioned elastic clamps—unless you enjoy littering stray mittens like confetti behind you. Cotton tights under a pair of overalls keep the wind out. For infants, snowsuit bags with attached mitts are the next best thing to staying home.

BUNT AND RUN TO FIRST

They're cozy, they're fuzzy, they're loose, and they're warm. If adults weren't afraid of looking like Barney, they'd wear buntings 24 hours a day. Buntings are great. They have slip-on mittens and footies. They're lightweight. And most are designed to accommodate car-seat harnesses. Buy big, so they'll last two winters.

FOOD AND BATH

It begins so calmly, with a weak suck. Then months of frantic bottle- or breast-snuffling give way to spoon-fed explorations. A thoughtful swallow followed by a raised eyebrow? Thumbs up. A scrunched-up face and a double head-fake? Thumbs down. Once a day, she emerges shimmering and sweet-smelling from the bath. Enjoy it. Mealtime—when your baby's face, to say nothing of your kitchen walls, looks like a Jackson Pollock—is inevitably just around the corner.

> "My mother didn't breast-feed me. She said she liked me as a friend."
>
> RODNEY DANGERFIELD

Nursing. Uniquely suited to the needs of a baby, mother's milk strengthens the immune system against infection, helps prevent allergies, and may even guard against infantile obesity. It is perhaps the most important preventive care you can give, even if you only do it for a short time. Nursing also gives your baby the most comforting moments of his early life. It isn't always easy. Build up your milk supply in the early weeks of breast-feeding by letting your baby nurse whenever he's hungry—at least every couple of hours during the day, on demand at night. Feeding takes anywhere from 20 minutes to an hour.

LATE-NIGHT WITH BABE

*Call a friend who lives in a different time zone.
Catch the second half of Attack of the Killer Tomatoes.
Call another friend who lives in a different time zone.
Reexamine your views on exactly how many months you need to breast-feed to qualify as a good mother.
Curse your husband's inability to lactate. Exult in his ability to bottle-feed.
Call an extremely tolerant friend who lives in the same time zone.*

Bottles. The bottle is much more than a feeding vessel. For breast-feeding mothers, it represents freedom, while someone else feeds the baby for a change. Introduce him to bottle-feeding as soon as he has mastered the breast—when he's two to four weeks old. Hold him close—he'll still want to feel you. Never prop a bottle in his mouth while he's in his crib—he could choke. Five minutes in boiling water will sterilize traditional bottles and nipples once they've been washed. Or run them through a hot dishwasher (catalogues sell bottle racks and nipple holders for dishwasher). Wash out bottles and sterilize after each feeding to be safe.

99 BOTTLES

Old-fashioned clear plastic bottles are straightforward. A newer style of holder has plastic disposable liners that let you expel all the air before feeding (good for colicky babies). Either way, if you're bottle-feeding exclusively, you'll need four 4-ounce bottles, and eight 8-ounce bottles, all with nipple units. Don't forget to buy liners if you use disposable bottles.

High Chairs. The one you were fed in was probably made of wood, with a sliding tray. It might work just fine for your baby—so long as it has a restraining belt, a dependable tray lock, good stability, and isn't covered in lead-based paint. Wheels are a plus so it can be a moveable feast. These are crucial qualities in a new chair as well. Look for one you don't have to assemble. Make sure you pick up a specially fitted cushion (baby stores and catalogues sell them) if it's got a hard seat. The tray should be easy to clean. In fact, feeding time can get pretty wild: you may want a chair you can toss in the shower. No kidding.

TIPPY CANOE AND TYLER TOO

You'll need rounded spoons small enough for little mouths (the tips can be rubberized for extra mouth protection).

Pretty baby china is great, but you can feed a baby out of anything that's clean. Don't buy it for yourself—it's a popular gift.

Sip-cups, a small evolutionary step backward from The Big Gulp, are great for mastering the art of drinking.

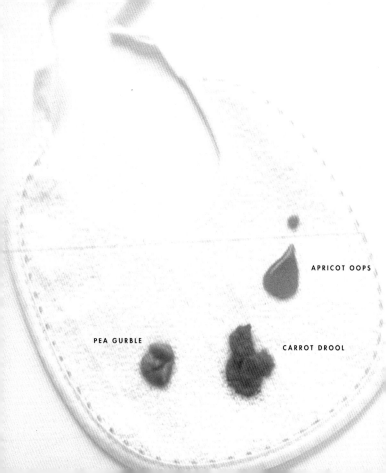

APRICOT OOPS

PEA GURBLE

CARROT DROOL

BIBBIDY-DO

If you like your child's clothes, you should own many bibs. Or at least several dish towels that can be tied so that they absorb what food your child does not. The average bib is terry cloth or molded plastic with a kind of gutter or a pocket at the bottom. Elastic mitten clips can double as fasteners for napkins if you find them easier to travel with than full-fledged bibs. As a rule, a bib should not be made of anything that is harder to wash than the piece of clothing it is meant to be protecting. In fact, fashion be damned: if you can simply wipe a bib off, so much the better.

Food. Making fresh baby food is simple—it's basically a matter of achieving the right texture. Smash bananas through a sieve, or mash them thoroughly with a fork and—presto—you've made lunch for your infant. The same technique works for other fruits and vegetables too, though when you start adding milk, cheese, yogurt, pasta, you name it, a small food grinder can come in handy. And remember that food allergies in children are thought to be the result of starting them on solid food too early. Wait until you doctor tells you it's all right.

DISH DECONSTRUCTIVISM
Lest you forget, dishes are not for food—they are for hurling through the air.
Think unbreakable (plastic). Look for ones with separate compartments
and suction cups or a bracket—to fix them to your baby's high-chair tray
when he's ready to try eating on his own.

Wash and Dry. Giving your newborn her first bath can be enough to give you your first heart attack. She's tiny, she's screaming, she's wriggly. Above all, she's wet and slippery. When do you attempt this terrifying activity? Not until the navel has healed and the umbilical cord has dropped off. Until then just damp-mop your infant while she's covered with a warm towel. Use an infant bathtub for the first few months. If you feel like filling up a real tub, keep the water level low and use a sponge seat to keep her from sliding around. Don't add to her fears by running the water while she's in the tub. Use a smaller, no-slip bath sponge.

49

Baby Soft. Infants need specially gentle products without a lot of chemicals and fragrances added. Most doctors will tell you not to overdo the baths (two or three a week is fine) and use very little, if any, soap. Shampoo should be no-tears baby shampoo. Baby oil can be helpful if your infant has cradle cap, but olive oil works just as well. Baby cornstarch, not baby powder, is a plus in hot, sticky weather but not necessary. Diaper-rash ointment is good to have around—though on newborns, rubbing breast milk on rashes works wonders. Petroleum jelly works for rubbing on the end of thermometers, but not for rashes. Diaper wipes should be alcohol-free. Newborns should just be cleaned with cotton and water. Sterile cotton balls are important for cleaning a newborn's eyes and cleaning the umbilical stump with alcohol. Baby nail clippers are slightly less terrifying to use than baby scissors, but either will do. Finally, a baby brush and comb may just be wishful thinking for a while, but eventually, they'll come in handy.

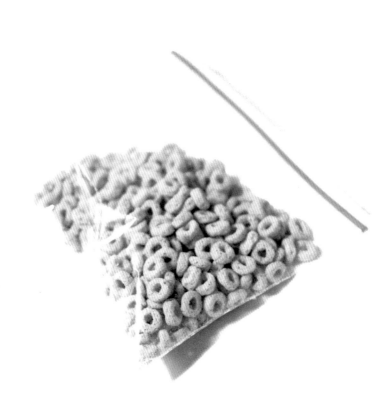

M O B I L E

"There are two classes of travel," Robert Benchley said. "First class, and with children." He's got a point. Vacations with babies can make you long for the relative calm of your job. Planning for a simple weekend away is more involved than preparing for an arctic trek. Still, the trade-off makes it worth the effort: you show your baby a new world, he shows you a new way of looking at it.

> "Ask your child what he wants for dinner only if he is buying."
>
> FRAN LEBOWITZ

OINTMENT

BLANKET

jaby Fresh

BABY WIPES

CHANGE OF
CLOTHES

PACIFIER

WASHCLOTH

LITTLE BIG BAG *It's a medical fact: diaper bag designers are incapable
of designing a good-looking, proper-sized diaper bag. A diaper bag should
have multiple compartments for extra diapers, wipes, Kleenex, a change of
clothes, little toys and books, food, bottles, and, of course, dirty diapers. It*

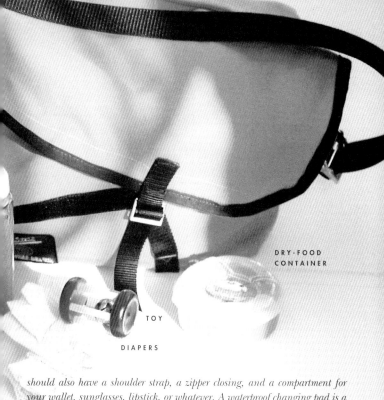

DRY-FOOD
CONTAINER

TOY

DIAPERS

should also have a shoulder strap, a zipper closing, and a compartment for your wallet, sunglasses, lipstick, or whatever. A waterproof changing pad is a plus. Keep the diaper bag packed so that you can just get up and go.

Snugli to Sassy. Monkeys do it, possums do it. Cole Porter never wrote a song about it, but baby carrying has been around for thousands of years—long before some child-product whiz came up with the nauseating term "Snugli." Studies have shown that babies who are carried cry less than babies who aren't. A large swatch of material can hold a baby securely to a parent's front, back, or side. Modern carriers come in several forms: a sling to hold a newborn close to the breast; an inward-facing carrier for infants and shy children; an outward-facing front carrier for babies who are curious about the world; a backpack for hiking, or going where no stroller can go.

CLIFFHANGER

These also go by the name "Sassy seats," after one of the brands on the market. They're great for restaurants and home use, if you don't have the space for a high chair. They fold up flat for easy storage and they make the baby feel like part of the action since she is literally at the table with you. A word of warning: They do not work on glass-top or pedestal tables, or shallow countertops.

Travel. The statistics are frightening: 700 kids per year are killed in car crashes; another 60,000 are injured. A car seat should be one of your first purchases whether or not you own a car. There are two basic types: rear-facing infant seats (good for babies weighing up to 20 pounds); and the more economical convertible models that can face the rear for the first few months, then be turned around (good up to 40 pounds). There are such a variety of harnesses that you'd think you were sending your baby into orbit, not simply trying to get to the supermarket safely. Bottom line: Get a car seat you find easy to use. It's the law.

CRIB NOTES

The perfect portable crib folds open in less than a minute. If it takes any longer, it's a portable headache. It should collapse neatly into a rectangular package measuring a foot high, a foot wide, and about 29 to 34 inches long. It can easily stand in for a playpen. Padding tends to be made out of nylon that cleans easily but rustles loudly whenever the baby moves. Wrapping a towel or quilted mattress pad around it under the fitted sheet quiets things down.

Hot Wheels. The first stroller you'll buy is a heavy combination carriage/stroller (16 to 28 pounds), with a fully reclining seat. The second is lightweight (7 to 14 pounds), and folds up into something smaller and less cumbersome than a bag of golf clubs. If you're an avid runner, you may also end up with a lightweight, three-wheeled runner's stroller. The issues? Safety: Check for restraint belts, brakes, stability, and a backup mechanism to keep the stroller from collapsing accidentally. View: Which way will your baby face—backward (looking at you) or forward (looking at the world)? Wheels: Should they be small and pivoting, or large and fixed? Style: Classic lines and navy blue dressing, or Maserati maneuverability and leopard-print audacity? Are you Mary Poppins or Elton John?

ROADSTER

The new hot rod on the block is the jogging stroller. It has large wheels and a long wheelbase that keep the stroller stable, and the sturdy metal frame can endure the long way home and more. Warning: Think twice about roller-blading with your tot—baby makes a lousy bumper.

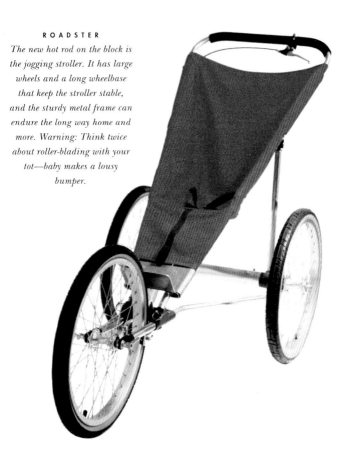

THE ROOM

It will smell—for better, and occasionally, for worse—like your baby. It will look like her too, the odd tiny sock lying on the floor, stuffed animals, the persistent red light of the intercom. It's where she will grow out of her first sweater and into her first pair of sneakers, where she'll sleep, dress, play, laugh, and scream. Your job is simply to make sure it's safe, comfortable, functional, and fun.

"People who say they sleep like a baby usually don't have one."

LEO BURKE

Sleep. Newborns sleep exactly as much as their bodies tell them to. You'll need a crib. The slats must be no more than $2\frac{3}{8}$ inches apart. The lowered dropside should be at least nine inches above the highest mattress setting. It should also be impossible for the baby to activate the dropside by herself. Pillows can suffocate—wait until she's strong enough to push them away. Keep night feedings short and sleepy. At six months, she'll sleep an average of 13 hours out of 24. At nine months, she'll fight sleep with everything she's got because it takes her away from you. Ease her into it with a bottle or a bedtime story.

MATTRESS

Look for firmness. Get a pocketed-coil innerspring or, if allergies are a problem, dense foam. A mattress should fit snugly in the crib, with no more than two adult finger widths between crib rails and mattress.

INTERCOM

Indispensable if your baby's room is out of earshot. Look for portability and safety: no exposed electrical parts. Remember to take it along when you travel. And no, that is not your six-month-old dispatching taxicabs to the airport—your intercom has just crossed signals with someone's cellular phone.

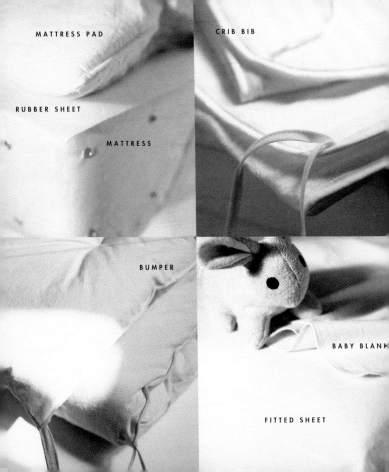

MATTRESS PAD

CRIB BIB

RUBBER SHEET

MATTRESS

BUMPER

BABY BLANK

FITTED SHEET

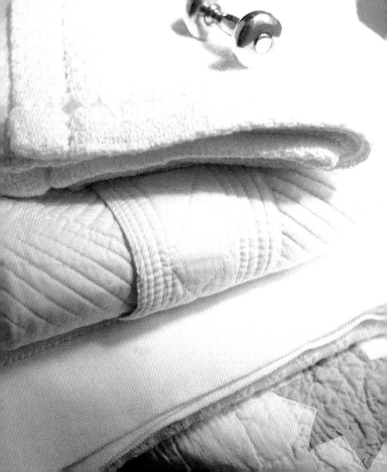

CHANGING TABLE

*Don't feel you need to spend a
fortune. Changing tables have one
very limited function. There are
three ready-made types—folding
ones with wheels, railed wooden
versions, and hinged chest
adapters. Convert an old bureau or
countertop by adding a standard
rubber pad with a fitted terry cloth
cover (you'll need at least two),
and some kind of protective
guardrail to the top. Just make sure
the height is comfortable for you.*

*Be sure to have the following
within easy reach: wastebasket;
diaper storage; diaper pail (if
you're using cloth diapers); baby
clothes; medicine and toiletry shelf
with a thermometer, Kleenex,
Q-Tips, Vaseline, diaper wipes,
A&D cream, Desitin, baby
cornstarch, and moisturizer.*

Holding Pens. They're ugly, they're made of plastic, and they're not cheap, but they'll allow you to put your baby down so you can eat a civilized meal once in a while. **INFANT SEATS.** Look for one that rocks, has a good handle, and is big enough to hold your baby for the first six months. Don't use it as a car seat. **INFANT BOUNCING SEATS.** Nice for when baby is three to six months old. Good for travel because they come apart. **SWING.** They're really ugly and take up a lot of space, but people with grouchy infants swear by them. **BABY BOUNCER.** They hang in the doorway, just high enough so that your baby can touch the floor and bounce. Most four-to-twelve-month-olds love them. **WALKERS.** Babies love them for that first taste of locomotion; safety-conscious guides like *Consumer Reports* don't. Should be used under careful supervision where bobsledding down a staircase is not an option. Contrary to its name, this product does nothing to help your baby walk.

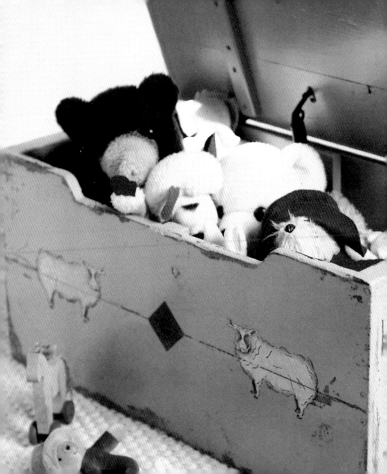

Storage. For such little people, babies accumulate a flabbergasting amount of stuff. Toy chests or plastic boxes in bright, primary colors hide a multitude of favorite—read: dog-eared and beat-up—objects. Buy a raw wood one and paint it yourself. Look for lightweight lids with safety closing mechanisms, or no lids at all. A medium-sized basket with handles makes carrying a choice selection of toys from room to room easier. Dust ruffles can look fussy, but they turn the dead space under a crib into storage. A small bureau—the one you're using for a changing space, perhaps—will hold most of your baby's clothes, though closet or shelf space for bulky snowsuits and clothes yet to be grown into is helpful. If you haven't got enough closet space, there are baby armoires with two drawers below hanging space. Keep any shelving unreachable from the crib and changing space. Unless they're bookshelves. Make sure they're low enough for her to reach the books herself.

Toys and Books. Get used to it: they'll be scattered underfoot like birdseed for the next decade or so. Who has more fun—the adult who buys the toy, or the kid who plays with it? Toys are amazing. Like the best teachers, they impart infinite skills—dexterity, hand-eye coordination, rhythm, reading skills, patience—without a trace of drudgery. Books made of indestructible substances make indelible marks on young imaginations—and pose special challenges to destruction-oriented infants. Remember: Anything can be a toy to a baby. Sometimes, the box ends up being more fascinating to him than the toy that comes in it.

GOODNIGHT BOOK
GOODNIGHT BABY
Even if your baby is too young to understand, get an early start on one of the best things about being a parent and read to her. It's a gift both of you can appreciate together—she discovers, you rediscover. You'll read her favorites a hundred times or more before the charm wears off and she's ready to move on. Not you, though. Pat the Bunny, Goodnight Moon, Where the Wild Things Are—*the words will become imprinted on your memory like a mantra.*

Decorating. Architect John Saladino once said, "A child's room should present the possibility of many environments." Babies are in constant need of new and more challenging stimuli. Make your design statements in ways that can easily be changed to fit his needs—not yours. He'll love contrast before he notices color—hang a black-and-white mobile you can exchange for a colored one when the time comes. You don't have to paint the walls with cute teddy bears and dancing alphabets. Why not keep them a calming backdrop to all the action? After all, sunlight filtering through a curtain will fascinate. Give your baby shapes and patterns that he can learn on things he can actually touch— sheets, pillows, bumpers, toys. And remember the limitlessness of his imagination: that small hooked rug on the floor is a future desert island. The rocking chair? A fort. That huge expanse of white wall? Perfect for his first Jean-Michel Basquiat imitations.

Fun and Functional. You've gotten the obvious out of the way. Now for the fun stuff—the perfectly proportioned furniture that makes your house look like a residence for Lilliputians. You remember the special chair you had as a child. The one that fit you like your favorite overalls—just right. Maybe you still have it to hand down. The arms weren't too wide, the seat wasn't too high, and the cushion had farm animals embroidered all over it. Enthroned, you were king or queen of all you surveyed. Kids connect to furniture that has been made just for them. Hold off on buying that bed shaped like a Ferrari—it'll get old fast. Ditto the life-sized stuffed grizzly bear. But a brightly painted desk and chair in a quiet corner feels like the right place to sit and draw. A make-believe kitchen or tool table can give a toddler a sense of empowerment. And tea sets let them pull you into the game—they've got the pot, so they're in control.

Memories. The accumulation seems to begin within minutes of birth, when you are handed your infant's footprint on a flimsy sheet of paper. From then on, you might as well accept your new job as Offical Record Keeper. Eventually, your video collection (her first burp!) will rival MTV's, and your collection of memorabilia (her dried-up umbilical cord!) the most rabid Elvis fan's. You may fill volumes of baby books with early triumphs, each one spelled out in Proustian detail. The avalanche of photos from the first month alone— get used to ordering double batches of prints—will have you assembling photo albums for the next year. Never mind; just do it! Things happen so fast that you'll find no moment is too small to remember.

"One of the disadvantages of having children is that they eventually get old enough to give you presents they make at school."

ROBERT BYRNE

The Checklists. There are moments when it seems that having a baby has nothing whatsoever to do with being a parent: it's really about making lists. Here are a few ready-made checklists. Add to them. Xerox them. Keep them with you. Do whatever it takes to calm that nagging suspicion that you might be forgetting something.

THINGS TO DO BEFORE BIRTH

1. Choose a pediatrician
2. Choose birth announcements
3. Think about a name
4. Prepare a list of phone numbers you will need at the hospital
5. Shop for food so there's some when you get home
6. Line up friends and family to help you out
7. Rest

MOVIES TO AVOID BEFORE BIRTH

The Battleship Potemkin
Rosemary's Baby
The Omen
Parenthood
The Joy Luck Club

TO TAKE TO THE HOSPITAL

1. Cash for the cab or parking garage
2. Watch or clock for timing contractions
3. Change for telephone calls
4. List of phone numbers
5. Insurance forms
6. Tennis ball to squeeze or use for counter-massage during labor
7. Sugarless lollipops to keep mouth from getting dry
8. Pair of socks in case your feet get cold
9. Washcloth
10. Walkman and calming tapes
11. Camera and film
12. Champagne, labeled with your name, for celebrating
13. Snacks for Dad

FOR YOUR ROOM

_ robe and 2 to 3 nursing
  nightgowns
_ slippers
_ toiletries and cosmetics
_ brush, hair dryer, etc.
_ glasses and contact lenses
_ books, magazines, or
  other distractions

FOR GOING HOME

_ a baggy, comfortable
  outfit to go home in
_ nursing bra
_ underwear
_ shoes, socks, hosiery
_ sweater or coat
_ shopping bags for gifts

FOR GOING HOME: BABY

_ 2 disposable diapers or 4
  cloth diapers with pins
  and wraps
_ onesie or T-shirt
_ 1 "stretchie"
_ socks or booties
_ 1 receiving blanket
_ sweater or cap if necessary
_ bunting or heavy blanket
_ car seat

SAFETY CHECKLIST

_ install smoke detectors
_ put safety plugs in all
  outlets
_ carpet the stairs to
  prevent slipping
_ install safety gates at the
  top and bottom of stairs
_ find out which house
  plants are poisonous—
  e.g., hyacinth bulbs,
  mistletoe—and keep them
  high up or out of the
  house entirely
_ check for easily swallowed
  objects on the floor
_ limit slips and falls with
  rubber-soled shoes or
  non-slip socks
_ tie venetian blind cords
  out of reach—they can
  strangle
_ watch all doors; keep glass
  doors open if possible
_ watch sharp edges and
  corners; soften them with
  corner cushions
_ anchor standing lamps,
  bookcases, heavy pictures
  and mirrors
_ install window guards and
  open windows from top
  when possible

_ do not leave plastic bags
  lying around—they can
  suffocate
_ watch for dangerous trash
  like throwaway razors,
  batteries, spoiled food
_ watch all heat sources
_ alcohol can be very toxic
  for children—lock it up
_ lock up all firearms (if you
  have to have them)
_ put latches on all cabinets
  or closets used for
  medicine, cleaning
  equipment, or liquor

MEDICINE CHEST

_ liquid aspirin substitute
  (Infants' Tylenol,
  Tempra, or Panadol)
_ liquefied charcoal (to
  induce vomiting if
  recommended by your
  local poison control
  bureau)
_ syrup of ipecac (also in
  case of accidental
  poisoning, but use only if
  advised by a doctor or
  poison expert)
_ liquid infant decongestant
  (use only if prescribed by
  a doctor)

_ antiseptic cream (baci-
tracin or neomycin for
minor scrapes and cuts)
_ hydrogen peroxide (for
cleaning cuts)
_ calamine lotion or
hydrocortisone cream
(1/2%) (for rashes and bug
bites)
_ rehydration fluid (if
doctor recommends it for
diarrhea)
_ baby sunscreen
_ rubbing alcohol (for
cleaning thermometers,
not for rubdowns)
_ calibrated spoon,
dropper, or oral syringe
(for giving medications)
_ Band-Aids
_ gauze and adhesive
_ tweezers
_ nasal aspirator (bulb
syringe to clear stuffy
noses)
_ cold-mist
vaporizer/humidifier
_ standard rectal
thermometer
_ small penlight (for
checking throat or pupils)
_ tongue depressors
_ heating pad and/or hot-
water bottle (for soothing
colic or relieving sore
muscles)

LINENS

_ 3 to 6 receiving blankets
_ 3 to 4 fitted sheets for
crib, bassinet, or carriage
_ 2 quilted mattress pads
_ 2 to 6 flannelized rubber
pads
_ 2 washable crib blankets
_ 1 washable blanket for
stroller
_ 2 to 3 terry-cloth hooded
bath towels
_ 2 to 3 washcloths
_ 1 dozen cloth diapers for
burping
_ hooded terry-cloth towel
soft washcloth
_ terry-cloth bath apron (to
keep bath giver dry)
_ no-slip bath sponge
_ padded faucet cover

LAYETTE CLOTHES

_ 6 onesies in 3- and 6-
month sizes ("onesies" are
better than plain
undershirts because they
don't ride up)
_ 3 to 4 diaper wraps (if
using cloth diapers)
_ 3 to 6 nightgowns with
drawstring bottoms
_ 2 to 3 zippered blanket
sleepers (for fall/winter)
_ 3 to 6 stretchy jumpsuits
with feet (for fall/winter)

_ 3 to 6 rompers (one-piece,
short-sleeved outfits for
spring/summer)
_ 2 to 3 pairs of booties or
socks
_ 2 washable bibs
_ 1 to 3 cotton cardigan
sweaters
_ 1 to 3 hats: lightweight
with brim for sun; heavier
weight with pull-down
flaps for ears in winter
_ 1 bunting with mitts or
snowsuit bag(for winter)

TRAVELING LIST

_ clothes for baby (consider
worst-case weather
scenarios)
_ diapers (enough to get
you through until you can
go to the store or wash a
load of cloth diapers)
_ bibs and burping cloths
_ toiletries: shampoo, soap,
moisturizer, nail clippers,
brush
_ medicines: Infants'
Tylenol, cold medicine,
thermometer, sunscreen
_ poison kit
_ diaper bag (see diaper
bag checklist for contents)
_ extra snacks and meals for
travel time

_ toy bag
_ favorite blanket or familiar object from crib
_ umbrella stroller
_ backpack
_ infant seat
_ portable crib with sheet, blanket, etc.
_ portable feeding seat
_ intercom

SUN

_ baby sunscreen
_ sun hat with brim
_ stroller parasol
_ thirst-quenching liquid and bottle
_ washcloth
_ light clothing that covers skin
_ baby sunglasses
_ roll-up sun shade for car

STROLLER ACCESSORIES

_ stroller cushion that ties on and has a hole for the restraining belt
_ movable sun parasol for sun protection and babies with light-sensitive eyes
_ mesh bag that attaches to the handles
_ stroller toys

DIAPER BAG LIST

_ diapers (take more than you think you'll need)
_ diaper wipes (handy for wiping hands and faces, as well as serving their more obvious function)
_ a changing pad (to protect furniture when you have to change your baby during a visit)
_ small plastic bags (for disposing of dirty diapers when there's no trash can around; for carrying home wet, soiled baby clothes; for snacks like Cheerios and cookies)
_ a bottle of boiled water (for baby to drink)
_ a formula feeding in case you're running late
_ a burping diaper
_ at least one change of clothes, depending on the length of the outing
_ an extra blanket or sweater—even in summer, to guard against air conditioning
_ a pacifier
_ a few toys or small books
_ sunscreen
_ snacks or jars of baby food for a meal; juice; fresh fruit, or dry cereal

LEAVE BEHIND FOR BABY-SITTER

_ go over everything he/she needs to know: feeding, sleeping, and play habits; burping and diapering information; calming tricks; give guided tour of clothes, kitchen, and medicine chest
_ phone number where you can be reached
_ list of crucial phone numbers (pediatrician, police, fire, poison control, grandparents, someone to call if you can't be reached); leave a copy of the list next to every phone in the house
_ be sure the house phone number is visibly printed on each phone
_ baby book with first-aid section
_ well-stocked medicine chest (not to be used without consulting doctor)
_ address of nearest emergency room
_ cab fare, in case of emergency

ACTIVITY CENTER

For Newborns:
_ high-contrast mobile
_ unbreakable mirror that attaches to crib rails
_ soft music
_ soft, brightly colored toys that make gentle sounds

For 1- to 3-month-olds:
_ images or books with high-contrast patterns
_ bright, varied, musical mobile
_ rattles
_ singing

For 4- to 7-month-olds:
_ soft balls
_ textured toys
_ toys with fingerholds
_ musical toys
_ see-through rattles

For 8- to 12-month-olds:
_ stacking toys
_ containers, pails, and cups
_ bath toys
_ blocks
_ "busy boxes" that open and make noise
_ squeeze toys
_ dolls or puppets
_ vehicle toys
_ balls
_ big picture books

_ push-pull toys
_ toy telephones

FAVORITE BOOKS

Babies:
Baby's First Words, by Lars Wik (Random House)
Baby's Mother Goose (cloth book), illustrated by Alice Schlesinger (Platt & Munk)
The Me Book (cloth book), by John E. Johnson (Random House)
Singing Bee! A Collection of Favorite Children's Songs, compiled by Jane Hart; illustrated by Anita Lobel (Lothrop, Lee and Shepard)
Eye Winker, Tom Tinker, Chin Chopper: 50 Musical Fingerplays, by Tom Glazer (Zephyr)
Where Is It? by Tana Hoban (Greenwillow)

Toddlers:
Early Words, by Richard Scarry (Random House)
Goodnight Moon, by Margaret Wise Brown (Harper & Row)
Marmalade's Nap, by Cindy Wheeler (Knopf)
Pat the Bunny, by Dorothy Kunhardt (Golden)

Sam Who Never Forgets, by Eve Rice (Puffin)
Shopping Trip, by Helen Oxenbury (Dial)
Taste the Raindrops, by Anna Hines (Greenwillow)
The Very Hungry Caterpillar, by Eric Carle (Philomel)
Where's My Baby? by H. A. Rey (Houghton Mifflin)
Where's Spot? by Eric Hill (Putnam)

RECOMMENDED READING FOR PARENTS

Caring for Your Baby and Young Child, by the American Academy of Pediatrics (Bantam Books)
Entertain Me! Creative Ideas for Fun and Games with Your Baby in the First Year, by The Riverside Mothers Group (Pocket Books)
Party Shoes to School and Baseball Caps to Bed, by Marilise Flusser (Simon & Schuster)
Your Baby and Child, by Penelope Leach (Knopf)
What to Expect the First Year, by Arlene Eisenberg, Heidi E. Murkoff, Sandee E. Hathaway, B.S.N. (Workman Publishing)

first aid.

Bringing up baby is, by definition, a flying-by-the-seat-of-your-pants proposition. But whether it's knowing how to live through a long car trip, nurse in public without causing traffic accidents, or calm a colicky child, here are a few tips to help you feel slightly more in control.

GROWTH AND DEVELOPMENT

2 months: tracks objects with eyes
2 to 3 months: first smiles
4 months: some head control; rolls over
6 months: sits up with support; abstract grabbing and raking gestures with hands
6 to 9 months: separation anxiety
9 months: sits up alone well; pincer grasp with thumb and index finger; plays peekaboo (understands concept of hidden objects)
9 to 12 months: crawls
12 months: walks; says maybe five possibly intelligible words
15 months: says 5 to 10 slightly more intelligible words

PARENT FURNITURE

At least one corner of the nursery should bear you in mind. Maybe it's by the window, with a view of the world outside. A comfortable rocking chair makes late-night nursing a little easier on the bones. Armrests are essential. A cushioned seat is nice—you may be there awhile. A footstool helps you get positioned better. A pillow to rest the baby on takes the weight off your arms. Put a reading light nearby, and a little table for bottles, books, or a comforting cup of tea.

SWIMMING

Your baby should have excellent head control before he is taken into a body of water. If he has any chronic infections, get the doctor's okay. Obviously, put off the swim if baby is sick. Never leave a child alone near water; drowning takes only seconds, even in an inch of water. For every baby or child, there should be at least one adult in the pool. Don't push him into anything that frightens him, and never submerge his face. Water should be comfortably warm—84° to 87° F. Exercise extreme care and strict supervision when using tubes, floaties, mattresses, or even swimsuits with built-in floats. Take toys out of the pool when not in use: they can be very tempting. Resuscitation techniques, infant CPR, and rescue equipment is scary to think about, but it could save your kid's life: learn how to use them. If possible, have a phone nearby for emergencies.

PLAYPENS

Playpens take up space, and some kids hate them. But they can be a safe place to put your baby if you need your hands free to do something else for a minute or two. (What a concept!) Wooden playpens are hard to find anywhere but at yard sales. If they're in good shape and meet a few safety standards—slats no more than 2⅜ inches apart; no lead-based paint or varnish; no sharp screws, nails, or rusty hinges—they're better than modern mesh ones, because babies can pull themselves up more easily. Mesh playpens are fine, but make sure they won't collapse and that the mesh is fine enough not to snag tiny fingers.

HOW TO WASH AND DRY

Get everything ready before you begin the bath. Water should be warm, with no bite—test it with your elbow or the inside of your wrist—and no more than 2 inches deep. Lower him gently, holding his head and neck firmly with one hand. Use the other hand to clean his eyes first—gently, with sterile cotton moistened with warm water. Use a fresh ball for each eye. Use a washcloth for his face, ears, and neck. Soap only his hands and diaper area. Rinse him thoroughly with a fresh washcloth. Wash his scalp with baby shampoo twice a week. Have a dry towel laid out on your lap. Lift him gently out of the water, place him on the towel, and swaddle him in it as you dry him off with a gentle, blotting motion.

MATTRESSES

Virtually all modern baby mattresses are plastic-coated. And with good reason: waste management is a skill most babies pick up sometime before they head for college. Flannelized rubber pads are still a good idea, and a regular cotton quilted mattress pad on top of that lets the baby's body breathe a little better and helps keep down sweating. If you're

*thinking of buying an old baby mattress,
know that any stains and smells that come
with it will also be yours—permanently. Once
the inside of an old mattress gets wet, there's
nothing you can do to prevent it from
becoming mildewed.*

CAR ACTIVITIES

1. *Parcel out the entertainment as you
   would water in a desert—slowly.*
2. *Hang toys within reach of your baby or
   strap an activity center to the back of the
   front seat or the bar of the car seat.*
3. *Play music and sing (just don't drive
   the driver crazy).*
4. *Older kids are great at entertaining
   little ones—borrow one for the ride.*
5. *Bring snacks.*
6. *Play peekaboo, and finger and toe games.*
7. *An awake baby will last up to an hour
   in a car seat before melting down.*
8. *Take breaks and let him move around,
   eat, play in a fast-food restaurant
   playground.*
9. *Plan to drive around the baby's sleep
   times. Nighttime is best for long trips.*

TIPS FOR TRAVEL

1. *If your baby has a favorite blanket or
   toy, be sure to bring it.*
2. *Travel entertainment should include
   an old toy—for familiarity and
   comfort—and a new one—for excitement
   and challenge.*

3. *Bring plenty of snacks and at least one
   meal in case you're delayed.*
4. *If you don't want to bring bibs, a
   clothespin will turn a restaurant napkin
   into a bib.*
5. *Travel at off-peak times when there will
   likely be empty seats for your baby to
   explore or stretch out on.*
6. *On planes, request the bulkhead seats; if
   not available, ask for aisle seats.*

DOCTOR'S VISITS

1. *2 weeks: first checkup*
2. *2 months, 4 months, 6 months: routine
   exam; weight and height check; shots:
   DTP (diphtheria, tetanus, pertussis
   vaccine), oral polio, hemophilus
   influenza vaccine)*
3. *9 months, 12 months: routine exam; first
   lead level test; blood test (for anemia);
   TB skin test*
4. *12 months: routine exam; urine screen;
   measles, mumps, rubella (MMR) shot;
   lead level test, blood test, and TB (if not
   done at 9 months)*
5. *15 months: routine exam; hemophilus
   influenza vaccine (MMR if not done at
   12 months)*
6. *18 months: routine exam; DTP and
   oral polio*
7. *24 months: routine exam; TB, lead
   level test, urine screen, and blood test
   (every year)*

EATING

4 to 6 months: first infant cereal
5 to 6 months: first pureed fruits
and vegetables
6 to 9 months: first pureed meats
9 to 12 months: eggs, milk products,
finger foods
12 months and on: well-cut-up foods;
honey, if allowed; shellfish

BURPING

Burp him every couple of ounces (if bottle-feeding) and every five minutes (if breast-feeding). Pat him gently on the back, or rub his back. Hold him against your shoulder, supporting buttocks with one hand while patting his back with the other. Or hold him facedown on your lap, stomach over one leg, head resting on the other. Or sit him up on your lap, supporting his upper chest and head with one hand, patting or rubbing his back with the other. Save yourself some laundry time: keep a burping cloth under his mouth (on your shoulder, your knee, or held under his mouth if he's in a sitting position). As any new dad who's watched a grandmother in action knows, infants are less fragile than they seem.

AVERAGE AGE FOR TOILET TRAINING

Studies have indicated that rushing toddlers into toilet training only prolongs the process. The average age is between 18 and 24
months, but some children take longer to get used to the idea. The important thing is that she wants to do it, not that you want her to. Stay relaxed. Let her get used to the potty before you try teaching her how to use it. Congratulate her when things go well; don't show your disappointment when they don't. Encourage her to use the potty before going to bed, and immediately after she wakes up. Your job is to make things as positive and unthreatening as possible.

CLIPPING NAILS

1. *Try doing it while your baby is asleep.*
2. *Use special baby nail scissors, with blunt tips.*
3. *Press finger pad out of the way before cutting.*
4. *Clippers may feel less scary: make sure they are small.*
5. *Emery boards take longer, but you can try filing down an infant's nails instead of cutting them.*
6. *If utensils make you nervous, try nibbling the nails off with your teeth.*

SLEEP

4 months: baby potentially capable of eating enough to sleep through the night. (Doesn't mean she will eat enough to make her sleep through the night.) Hard to chart. Varies wildly with every baby.

LEAD INFORMATION

1. *EPA hotline: 800/426-4791*
2. *Sources of lead contamination include: old paint chips, certain crayons, drinking water that flows through lead pipes, soil, newspapers and magazines (if ingested)*
3. *Increase resistance to lead with good nutrition: give your baby adequate iron and calcium, filter contaminated water, and switch baby to bottled water.*

COLIC

1. *Try to comfort the baby as much as you can by holding and carrying her; rocking; humming as you hold her.*
2. *Swaddle her.*
3. *Take her for a ride in the stroller or car.*
4. *Learn "colic holds" that put light pressure on her stomach; find her favorite position.*
5. *Learn gentle stomach massage and other stroking techniques.*
6. *Give her a warm bath.*
7. *Give her a pacifier—sucking can be comforting to a crying baby.*
8. *Give her to someone else to hold.*
9. *Give yourself a break, even if you have to put her down in her crib for a minute while you take a shower or tune out for ten minutes.*
10. *Call for help from a friend.*
11. *Get some exercise to work off your tension.*
12. *Talk about it.*

NURSING IN PUBLIC

1. *Department store lounges are often quiet and comfortable.*
2. *Get away from the crowd.*
3. *Shirts and dresses with special flaps are available; otherwise, be sure you're in something that can be unbuttoned or unsnapped easily.*

EQUIPMENT

Nursing bras—shop around for one that doesn't make you look too much like a Valkyrie. Button-down shirts make discretion possible when nursing in public. Breast pumps are odd—who really likes the idea of vacuuming liquid from her bosom?—but essential if you plan on being away from your baby for more than a few hours. Drugstores and hospitals rent large, efficient electric pumps that work the quickest. You can also buy battery-operated and handheld electric pumps at most drugstores, but they're not too speedy.

where. A Chic Simple store looks out

on the world beyond its shopwindow. Items are practical and comfortable and will work with pieces bought elsewhere. The store can be a cottage industry or a global chain, but even with an international vision it is still rooted in tradition, quality, and value.

FREEDOM OF CHOICE

Even as the world shrinks and chain stores expand globally, there are plenty of locales where choice is limited if there is any choice at all. However, most manufacturers today can aid you in finding a store or even mail direct to you. The U.S. numbers listed below will help give you freedom of choice.

Baby Gap/Gap Kids	800/333-7899
Kids R Us	800/543-7787
Oshkosh B'Gosh	800/282-4674
Walden Kids	800/243-7510
Department of Transportation	800/424-9393
Dept. NEF 10, Washington, DC 20590	
(For recall or other information on infant/toddler car seats)	
Womb with a View	
available through International Micro Designs, Inc.	916/686-8074
8705 Elk Grove Boulevard, Elk Grove, CA 95624	
(First computerized pregnancy information program provides	
weekly updates about the normal development of	
mother and fetus)	

United States

CALIFORNIA

BERKELEY DESIGN
SHOP & KIDS' ROOM
2970 Adeline Street
Berkeley, CA 94703
510/652-3398
(*Children's furniture*)

JONATHAN-KAYE BY
COUNTRY LIVING
3548 Sacramento Street
San Francisco, CA 94118
415/563-0773
(*Nursery furniture*)

MACY'S UNION SQUARE
170 O'Farrell Street
San Francisco, CA 94102
415/397-3333

COLORADO

GERRY BABY
PRODUCTS CO.
12520 Grant Drive
Denver, CO 80220
800/362-3200
(*Frame carrier*)

CONNECTICUT

CANDY NICHOLS
68 Greenwich Avenue
Greenwich, CT 06830
203/622-1220, call for
locations in New Canaan,
CT; Rye, NY; and
Edgartown, MA
(*Clothes for babies*)

LITTLE LACEY
CUSTOM CHILDREN'S
WEAR
268 Mason Street
Greenwich, CT 06830
203/861-0101
(*Coordinated accessories and
layettes, newborns to size 8*)

OOPS
700 Canal Street
Stamford, CT 06902
203/358-0628
(*Designer outlet for children's
clothing*)

ZOOM
1051 Long Ridge Road
Stamford, CT 06903
203/322-0063
(*Children's clothing*)

MICHIGAN

GENERATIONS/THE
CHILDREN'S STORE
337 South Main Street
Ann Arbor, MI 48104
313/662-6615
(*Children's clothes, toys,
books, and music*)

NEW YORK

BUNNIES CHILDREN'S
DEPT. STORE
969 Central Park Avenue
Scarsdale, NY 10583
914/723-2003
(*Baby clothing and furniture*)

COTTONTAILS
76 Purchase Street
Rye, NY 10580
914/921-4042
(*Natural fiber baby clothing*)

COUNTRY GEAR LTD.
Main Street
Bridgehampton, NY 11932
516/537-1032
(*English country furniture*)

DARLING FURNITURE
137 East Post Road
White Plains, NY 10601
914/949-6777 or
800/360-BABY for other
New York locations
(Baby furniture and strollers)

DESIGNER KIDS/
FAMILY DISCOUNT
CENTER
719 North Bedford Road
Bedford Hills, NY 10507
914/666-6660
(Baby clothing and supplies)

KIDDIE KING
84-86 Mamaroneck Avenue
White Plains, NY 10601
914/948-8313
(Baby clothing and strollers)

ONE-TO-GROW, INC.
1855 East Main
Peekskill, NY 10566
914/737-2115
(Baby and preemie clothing)

RYE SHOE STORE
39 Purchase Street
Rye, NY 10580
914/967-1643
(Shoes)

TWINKLE TOES
152 Larchmont Avenue
Larchmont, NY 10538
914/833-1455
(Infant clothes and bedding)

UNCLE LEW'S TOYS
67 Purchase Street
Rye, NY 10580
914/921-1570
(Toys, cards, stationery)

New York City

ABC CARPET AND
HOME
888 Broadway
New York, NY 10003
212/473-3000
(Home furnishings)

AD HOC SOFTWARES
410 West Broadway
New York, NY 10012
212/925-2652
(Bed and bath accessories)

ALBEE'S
715 Amsterdam Avenue
New York, NY 10025
212/662-8902
(Baby clothing and supplies)

BABY PALACE
181 Seventh Avenue
New York, NY 10011
212/924-3700
(Baby clothing and supplies)

BARNEYS NEW YORK
106 Seventh Avenue
New York, NY 10011
212/929-9000
(Baby clothing and furniture)

BELLINI JUVENILE
FURNITURE
1305 Second Avenue
New York, NY 10021
212/517-9233
(Baby clothing and furniture)

BEN'S FOR KIDS, INC.
1380 Third Avenue
New York, NY 10021
212/794-2330
(Baby clothing and supplies)

BERGDORF GOODMAN
754 Fifth Avenue
New York, NY 10019
212/753-7300
(Silver baby cups and baby
clothing)

THE CHOCOLATE SOUP
946 Madison Avenue
New York, NY 10021
212/861-2210
(Handmade clothing and toys)

C.I.T.E. DESIGN
100 Wooster Street
New York, NY 10012
212/431-7272
(Antique American furniture)

CITY KIDS
130 Seventh Avenue
New York, NY 10011
212/620-0906
(Baby clothing, supplies, toys)

CRABTREE & EVELYN
1310 Madison Avenue
New York, NY 10128
212/289-3923
(Soaps and body cream)

DAFFY'S
111 Fifth Avenue
New York, NY 10003
212/599-4477
(Discount baby clothing)

DISTANT ORIGIN
153 Mercer Street
New York, NY 10012
212/941-0024
(Rustic furnishings)

EASTERN MOUNTAIN
SPORTS
601 Broadway
New York, NY 10012
212/505-9860
(Snuglis and baby backpacks)

E.A.T. GIFTS
1062 Madison Avenue
New York, NY 10028
212/861-2544
(Unique baby items)

THE ENCHANTED
FOREST
85 Mercer Street
New York, NY 10012
212/925-6677
(Beasts, books, handmade
toys)

ENTRÉE LIBRE
110 Wooster Street
New York, NY 10012
212/431-5279
(Chairs and other original
home furnishings)

GREENSTONES
442 Columbus Avenue
New York, NY 10024
212/580-4322
(Baby clothing)

GUGGENHEIM MUSEUM
SOHO
575 Broadway
New York, NY 10012
212/423-3876
(Children's art books)

HUSH-A-BYE
1459 First Avenue
New York, NY 10021
212/988-4500
(Clothing, furniture, strollers)

JULIAN & SARA
103 Mercer Street
New York, NY 10012
212/226-1989
(Baby clothing and toys)

KATE'S PAPERIE
561 Broadway
New York, NY 10012
212/941-9816
(Paper goods)

KIDDING AROUND
68 Bleecker Street
New York, NY 10012
212/598-0228
(Baby clothing, supplies, toys)

KIDS' DIGS
215 West 79th Street
Suite 1A
New York, NY 10024
212/787-7800
(Architect/interior design,
specializing in environments
for children)

KIDZOWN
336 First Avenue
New York, NY 10009
212/677-0604
(Baby and preemie clothing)

KIEHL'S
109 Third Avenue
New York, NY 10003
212/475-3400 or
800/933-4656
*(Pediatrician-tested baby skin-
care and shampoo products)*

MOM'S NIGHT OUT
970 Lexington Avenue
New York, NY 10021
212/744-MOMS
Appointment preferred
*(High fashion maternity wear
for rent)*

NANNYTAX
50 East 42nd Street
Suite 2108
New York, NY 10017
212/867-1776
*(Complete tax service for
employers of domestic help)*

**PATTERSON, FLYNN,
MARTIN, INC.**
979 Third Avenue
New York, NY 10022
(Carpets and rugs)

**PEANUTBUTTER &
JANE**
617 Hudson Street
New York, NY 10014
212/620-7952
(Infant and preemie clothing)

PENNY WHISTLE TOYS
132 Spring Street
New York, NY 10012
212/925-2088
(Infant and children's toys)

PORTICO KIDS
1167 Madison Avenue
New York, NY 10028
212/717-1963
(Kids' furniture)

**SAFETY-NET
CHILDPROOFING, INC.**
2166 Broadway, Suite 7E
New York, NY 10024
212/496-6303
(Professional childproofers)

SHOOFLY
465 Amsterdam Avenue
New York, NY 10024
212/580-4390
(Children's shoes)

SMALL CHANGE
964 Lexington Avenue
New York, NY 10021
212/772-6455
(Children's wear, infants)

SPACE KIDDETS
46 East 21st Street
New York, NY 10010
212/420-9878
(Baby clothing and toys)

SPRING FLOWERS
410 Columbus Avenue
New York, NY 10021
212/721-2337
(Baby clothing)

TERRA VERDE
120 Wooster Street
New York, NY 10012
212/925-4533
(Natural linens and soaps)

TUTTI BAMBINI
1490 First Avenue
New York, NY 10021
212/472-4238
(Baby clothing and toys)

WEST SIDE KIDS
498 Amsterdam Avenue
New York, NY 10024
212/496-7282
(Baby toys)

WICKER GARDEN'S
CHILDREN
1327 Madison Avenue
New York, NY 10128
212/410-7001
(Baby clothing and furniture)

ZITOMER
969 Madison Avenue
New York, NY 10021
212/737-4480
(Baby and preemie clothing)

ZONA
97 Greene Street
New York, NY 10012
212/925-6750
(Children's furniture and books)

WASHINGTON

RACING STROLLERS,
INC.
2609 River Road
Yakima, WA 98902
800/241-1848 for free
brochure or name of dealer
near you

WISCONSIN

OLSEN'S MILL DIRECT
1641 South Main Street
Oshkosh, WI 54901
414/426-6360
(Oshkosh B'Gosh children's
wear at discount)

NATIONAL
LISTINGS

BABY SUPERSTORE, INC.
605 Haywood Road
Greenville, SC 29607
803/675-0299
(For the complete nursery)

EARTH'S BEST BABY
FOOD
4840 Pearl East Circle
Suite 201E
Boulder, CO 80301
800/442-4221
(Organically grown baby food)

F.A.O. SCHWARZ
767 Fifth Avenue
New York, NY 10153
212/644-9400
(Toys and stuffed animals)

GYMBOREE
700 Airport Boulevard
Suite 200
Burlingame, CA 94010
415/579-0600 for store
nearest you
(Baby clothing and more)

TIFFANY & CO.
727 Fifth Avenue
New York, NY 10022
800/526-0649
(From baby announcements to
silver baby accessories)

CATALOGUE AND
MAIL ORDER

DYVINITY
P.O. Box 683
Franklin Park, NJ 08823
800/842-0392
(Handmade christening
wear)

HANNA ANDERSON
1010 Northwest Flanders
Street
Portland, OR 97209-3199
800/346-6040
(Clothes for mother and baby)

POTTERY BARN
Mail Order Department
P.O. Box 7044
San Francisco, CA 94120
800/922-5507
(Home furnishings)

IKEA
1000 Center Drive
Elizabeth, NJ 07202
908/289-4488 or
412/747-0747 for East
Coast listings or 818/842-
4532 for West Coast listings
(Baby furniture)

THE RIGHT START
CATALOGUE
5334 Sterling Center Drive
Westlake Village, CA 91361
800/526-5220 or
818/707-7100
(Children's clothing)

INTERNATIONAL LISTINGS

France

PARIS

AU NAIN BLEU
408, rue St.-Honoré
75008
42/60-39 01
(The F.A.O. Schwarz of Paris)

BONNICHON
7, avenue Victor-Hugo
75016
45/01-70-17
(Traditional baby furniture)

BONPOINT
15, rue Royale
75008
47/42-52-63
(Classic children's clothes)

FORMES
5, rue du Vieux-Colombier
75006
45/49-09-80
(Maternity clothes in fine-quality fabrics)

MIKI HOUSE
1, rue du Vieux-Colombier
75006
46/33-77-55
(Upscale Japanese children's brand clothing for ages 0 to 8)

NAJ-OLEARI
1-bis, rue du Vieux-Colombier
75006
40/46-00-43
(Clothes for babies in whimsical motifs)

PETIT BATEAU
72, avenue Victor-Hugo
75016
45/00-13-95
(100% cotton babies' pajamas and underwear)

POM D'API
28, rue du Four
75006
45/48-39-31
(Inventive shoes for children)

TERRITOIRE
30, rue Boissy d'Anglais
75008
42/66-22-13
(Children's boutique of French toys and games)

Great Britain

HEREFORD

WILLEY WINKLE
Offa House, Offa Street
HR1 2LH
432/268-018
(Handmade baby cot mattresses with natural flame-retardant lambswool)

LONDON

ANTHEA MOORE EDE
16 Victoria Grove
W8 5RW
71/584-8826
(Children's clothes)

CRECHENDO
St. Luke's Hall
Adrian Mews, Ifield Road
SW10
71/259-2727 for color brochure and information
(Play gyms, with centers across London)

HAMLEYS
188 Regent Street
W1
71/734-3161
(Toys)

MOTHERCARE
(Head Office)
Cherry Tree Road
Watford
WD2 5SH
0923 241000
(Maternity and baby clothing)

**SOUTH
HUMBERSIDE**

FUN-GAREES BY BRIC-
A-BRATS
Flapsdown, Top Farm
Elsham
DN20 0NX
652/688-712 for brochure
*(Practical and fun clothes for
babies in 100% cotton)*

WEST SUSSEX

KIDDIPROOF, HAGO
PRODUCTS LTD.
Durban Road
Bognon Regis
PO22 9RD
243/863-131 for
information
*(A total range of child home
safety products)*

Italy

ROME

AL SOGNO
Piazza Navona 53
00168
686/41-98
(Stuffed animals and toys)

CITTÀ DEL SOLE
Via della Scrofa 65
00168
687/54-04
(Educational toys and games)

Japan

OSAKA

TEN MONTHS
1-8 12 Kosakahonmachi
Higashi-Osaka-shi 577
06/730-5140
(Baby clothes and bedclothes)

TOKYO

AKACHAN HONPO
106017 Nihonbashi-
Bakurocho
Chuo-ku 103
03/3661-6621
*(Wholesale store for maternity
and baby goods)*

GINZA FAMILIAR
6-10-16 Ginza
Chuo-ku 104
03/3574-7111
*(Department store for babies
and kids)*

HAPPY BELL
1-26-20 Jiyugaoka, 2nd Floor
Meguro-ku 152
03/3724-3018
*(Maternity and baby goods
boutique)*

KIDS FARM PAO
1-22-14 Jin-nan
Shibuya-ku 150
03/5458-0111
(Department store for kids)

MAMA'S ET PAPA'S
1-16-4 Tomigaya
Shibuya-ku 151
03/3469-6410
(Nursery furnishings)

TUTTO CHICCO
2-10-18 Jiyugaoka
Meguro-ku 152
03/5701-1101
*(Maternity and baby clothing
from Italy)*

RESOURCES

ACKNOWLEDGMENTS

MANUFACTURER & RETAIL RESEARCH	Susan Claire
QUOTE RESEARCH	Lige Rushing and Kate Doyle Hooper
COPY EDITING	Borden Elniff

AND SPECIAL THANKS TO: Amy Capen, Tony Chirico, M. Scott Cookson, Bia Da Costa, Lauri Del Commune, Michael Drazen, Sally Swift Faunce, Deborah Freeman, Jane Friedman, Janice Goldklang, Jo-Anne Harrison, Patrick Higgins, Katherine Hourigan, Andy Hughes, Carol Janeway, Barbara Jones-Diggs, Nicholas Latimer, William Loverd, Kelsey Malloy, Anne McCormick, Dwyer McIntosh, Sonny Mehta, Amy Needle, Joanna Needle, Lan Nguyen, Candy Nichols, Maggie O'Brien of Wilhelmina/Wee Willys Models, Inc., Julian Richards, Lauren Shakely, Anne-Lise Spitzer, Dylan Stone, Morgan Stone, Robin Swados, Aileen Tse, Shelley Wanger.

COMMUNICATIONS

The world has gotten smaller and faster but we still can only be in one place at a time, which is why we are anxious to hear from you. We would like your input on stores and products that have impressed you. We are always happy to answer any questions you have about items in the book, and of course we are interested in feedback about Chic Simple.

Our address is:

84 WOOSTER STREET • NEW YORK, NY 10012

fax **(212) 343-9678**

Our email address: **info@chicsimple.com**

Compuserve number: **72704,2346**

P.S. If you like the **DIAPER BAG** pictured on **PAGES 54-55** give us a call. We have a limited number in stock; it is truly magical.

Stay in touch because "The more you know, the less you need."

KIM JOHNSON GROSS AND JEFF STONE

TYPE

The text of this book was set in two typefaces: New Baskerville and Futura. The ITC version of **NEW BASKERVILLE** is called Baskerville, which itself is a facsimile reproduction of types cast from molds made by John Baskerville (1706–1775) from his designs. Baskerville's original face was one of the forerunners of the typestyle known to printers as the "modern face"—a "modern" of the period A.D. 1800. **FUTURA** was produced in 1928 by Paul Renner (1878–1956), former director of the Munich School of Design, for the Bauer Type Foundry. Futura is simple in design and wonderfully restful in reading. It has been widely used in advertising because of its even, modern appearance in mass and its harmony with a great variety of other modern types.

SEPARATION AND FILM PREPARATION BY
DIGITAL PRE-PRESS, INC.
New York, New York

PRINTED AND BOUND BY
BERTELSMANN PRINTING AND MANUFACTURING CORP.
Berryville, Virginia

HARDWARE

Apple Macintosh Quadra 700 and 800 personal computers; APS Technologies Syquest Drives; MicroNet DAT Drive; SuperMac 21" Color Monitor; Radius PrecisionColor Display/20; Radius 24X series Video Board; Hewlett-Packard LaserJet 4, Supra Fax Modem

SOFTWARE

QuarkXPress 3.3, Adobe Photoshop 2.5.1, Microsoft Word 5.1, FileMaker Pro 2.0, Adobe Illustrator 5.0.1

MUSICWARE

Child to Child (*Instrumental Lullabies of the World*), Holly Hunter Reads (*The Three Billy Goats, Three Little Pigs*), Carly Simon (*Bells, Bears & Fishermen*), John McCutcheon (*Family Garden*), Audrey Hepburn (*Enchanted Tales*), Ella Jenkins (*This Is Rhythm*), Put On Your Green Shoes (*An Album Dedicated to Healing the Planet*), Michael Feinstein (*Pure Imagination*), Marlo Thomas (*Free To Be You and Me*), Lady Smith Black Mambazo (*Gift of the Tortoise*), David Grisman/Jerry Garcia (*Not for Kids Only*), The Manhattan Transfer (*Tubby the Tuba*), Taj Mahal (*Smilin' Island of Song*), Weird Al/Wendy Carlos (*Peter and the Wolf*), Disney (*For Our Children*), Greg Brown (*Bath Tub Blues*), Vince Goraldi Trio (*A Charlie Brown Christmas*).

"To be simple is the best thing in the world; to be modest is the next best thing. I am not so sure about being quiet."

G . K . CHESTERTON

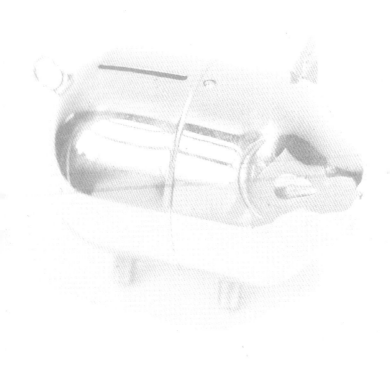